DOLPHINS

P9-DME-226

Wildlife Monographs – Dolphins
Copyright ©2007 Evans Mitchell Books

Text copyright ©2007 Jonathan Bird
Photographs copyright ©2007 Jonathan Bird
Except pages: 4, 9, 14, 17, 18, 20, 22, 26, 40, 43, 44,
50, 54, 68, 70, 73, 74, 83, 86, 94 Copyright ©2007
Brandon Cole

Jonathan Bird has asserted his rights to be identified
as the author and photographer of this work in
accordance with Section 77 of the Copyright, Designs
and Patents Act 1988

First published in the United Kingdom by:
Evans Mitchell Books
Norfolk Court, 1 Norfolk Road,
Rickmansworth, Hertfordshire WD3 1LA
United Kingdom

Jacket and Book Design by:
Roy Platten
Eclipse
roy.eclipse@btopenworld.com

All rights reserved. No part of this publication may be
reproduced, stored in a retrieval system or transmitted
in any form or by any means; electronic, mechanical,
photocopying or otherwise, without the prior written
consent of the publisher

British Library Cataloguing in Publication Data.
A CIP record of this book is available on request
from the British Library.

ISBN: 1-901268-17-9
      978-1-901268-17-1

Pre Press: F.E Burman, London, United Kingdom

Printed in Thailand

DOLPHINS

JONATHAN BIRD

Evans Mitchell Books

Contents

In British Columbia, a small pod of
Pacific White-sided dolphins
(Lagenorhynchus obliquidens) jump
playfully alongside the boat.

Introduction

Dolphins have been a part of human history in the form of myths and folklore since the beginning of recorded time. The ancient Greeks believed dolphins had spiritual properties, and in Greek law, it was illegal to harm a dolphin in any way. According to Greek myth, Apollo once took the form of a pod of dolphins to lead a lost ship from Crete. In gratitude, the sailors vowed to serve the oracle of Apollo, but renamed it Delphi in honor of the form he took in saving them. Hence, the famous Greek oracle of Delphi is named after dolphins. In fact, there are legends about dolphins helping humans in many different cultures from ancient to modern. Dolphins appear on cave drawings in Norway dated from 2200 BC.

Above: A pair of Bottlenosed dolphins (*Tursiops truncatus*) jump out of the water, showing the grace associated with this common species of dolphin.

Opposite page: The Bottlenosed dolphin has been demonstrated to be extremely intelligent—perhaps more than monkeys and apes.

Perhaps because of the television series "Flipper" we identify dolphins as intelligent and friendly. Research has shown that they are social animals, living together in groups called pods. Many dolphins in captivity have died seemingly just from loneliness. Pods of dolphins are amazingly playful. Why do they ride in the bow waves of boats? Most people believe they do it just for fun. They get a push from the pressure wave and surf along with almost no effort, frequently jumping out of the water.

Below: Atlantic Spotted dolphins (Stenella frontalis), here photographed in the Bahamas, are one of the species most willing to interact with divers and snorkelers. Their curiosity drives them to investigate things out of the ordinary.

Opposite page: Many species of dolphins love to bow ride. These Pacific White-Sided dolphins get a free ride on the bow of a boat. It's like surfing for the dolphins, and fun for people to watch as well!

If humans have a counterpart in the sea, a creature of high intelligence, with a social order, and the ability to reason, dolphins are it. Unfortunately, humans invade the world of dolphins in many ways. We still hunt and kill them, often in the pursuit of goals valuable only to us. We have entrapped them and forced them to perform. Now the pollution we dump into the seas may create the greatest threat the dolphins have ever had to face. Evidence suggests that the build up of certain biopersistent toxins could be impairing dolphins' immune systems and fertility. Dead dolphins wash up on beaches all the time, the victims of pollution or mysterious ailments that we cannot explain.

Many countries have created laws to protect marine mammals, but these laws are primarily applied to the protection of the large whales. Dolphins are regularly slaughtered in many countries, notably Japan, with impunity. They are killed not just as food, but sometimes because they are believed to interfere with fishing practices, or because they are believed to compete with man for food.

Every year, millions of people get a close look at dolphins on whale watching trips. This popular form of tourism has given people a new-found appreciation for these amazing citizens of the seas. It is one thing to read about dolphins in a book, but quite another to see one in person, in the wild.

Perhaps someday we will live in a world where we will live at peace with our counterparts in the seas and perhaps we will be able to understand what dolphins may be able to teach us. We can only hope that as we continue to better understand and appreciate dolphins, we will come to realize that they should be cherished and fully protected the world over.

Previous page: Bottlenosed dolphins may not appear that large, but they reach almost 4 metres and 650 kg! A newborn is around a metre long.

Right: Spotted dolphins often play follow the leader, where one animal leads the way and others follow behind in chase. In the warm waters of the Bahamas, this group races towards the sunlit surface for a breath.

Overleaf: In the San Juan Islands of Washington state, a whale-watching boat keeps a safe distance from a pod of Orcas. Whale watching is big business, and many countries have learned that whales and dolphin are worth more to the tourist trade than they are as food.

Natural History

At first glance, a dolphin may not seem to bear much resemblance to ourselves, but the similarities between humans and dolphins are striking. On the taxonomic scale, we are both mammals, a class of vertebrates sharing many characteristics. For example, we are both warm blooded, bear live young, and feed our young milk. Even more obvious, we both have lungs and breathe air. A dolphin might look like a fish, but it has a lot more in common with humans than with fish.

We share other traits which go beyond simple taxonomy. We both care for and protect our offspring for a fairly long time. We both have a social system involving friends and families. We are both the most intelligent animals in our respective worlds. Yet, in spite of our intelligence, we actually know very little about dolphins.

Above: The False Killer whale *(Pseudorca crassidens)* is a large dolphin that reaches 6 metres long and is often known to be rather aggressive. It even feeds on other dolphins at times, though it seems to prefer fish. These tropical animals can be curious though, sometimes approaching boats, and, occasionally, divers. I never felt threatened by these animals as they buzzed me a few times for a look.

Opposite page: The Orca *(Orcinus orca)* sometimes called the "Killer whale" is actually the largest member of the dolphin family, reaching almost 10 metres in length and 9 tons in weight. Nobody is completely sure why they breach (jump out of the water) but it could be to communicate, to frighten fish, or just for fun. At 9 tons, they make quite a splash!

From the fossil record, we know that all members of the order *Cetacea* (whales and dolphins) evolved from four-legged land mammals about a hundred million years ago, long before humans walked the earth. From those early beginnings, the early cetaceans adapted to their aquatic environment through millions of years of evolution. It is believed that the ancestors of whales and dolphins began their migration to the sea by foraging for food and hunting in the shallows near shore, using legs to walk and swim. Over time, they slowly lost their hind limbs, while their tail evolved into a fluke. The fingers or toes on their front limbs became webbed, eventually metamorphosing into the flippers we see today. Still, the present day skeleton of whales and dolphins contains finger bones left over from those ancient lost fingers.

The nose moved from the front of the head to the top, becoming a blowhole.

Previous page: A lively dolphin that loves to jump as it swims, the Pacific White-Sided dolphin lives in the cooler waters of the north Pacific. The body coloration varies slightly from individual to individual.

Above: Risso's Dolphins *(Grampus griseus)* often have scars all over their bodies from fighting with each other. Males use their teeth to scratch other individuals when fighting over females. As the animals age, they get whiter in color like the animal in the foreground.

Opposite page: Off Hawaii, a Short-finned Pilot whale *(Globicephala macrorhynchus)* is hanging vertically in the water column, staring at me. Normally, these animals (which are actually large dolphins) are shy and hard to approach underwater. But a large pod of these animals was being bothered by a pod of hyperactive Melon-headed whales, and the distraction made the Pilot whales unconcerned with my presence.

Overleaf: A Long-snouted Spinner dolphin doing what it does best – jumping out of the water and spinning! This is a tropical dolphin, found around the world in warm water.

As time went on, the whales specialized in feeding on different prey. Eventually the whales branched off into two different groups. One group kept its teeth, becoming what we call the *Odontoceti* (or "toothed") whales. Today, the suborder *Odontoceti* includes all the toothed whales, such animals as the Sperm whale, the Orca and the Bottlenosed dolphin. Some people find it surprising to learn that dolphins are just small, toothed whales. These toothed whales feed on prey using their sharp teeth.

Above: This pod of Melon-headed whales *(Peponocephala electra)* are actually tropical dolphins that love bow wave riding. They do not approach divers readily.

Opposite page, top: A Bottlenosed dolphin takes a quick breath at the surface through the blowhole on the top of its head.

Opposite page, bottom: A Long-snouted Spinner dolphin is on the move.

Overleaf: A pod of Orcas on the hunt. While some Orcas earned the nickname "Killer whales" for voraciously hunting large mammals like seals and whales, most actually eat fish. Using their powerful tails, Orcas can stun fish by smacking the water very hard near a school of fish.

The other group of ancestral whales found a different niche in the food chain. Exploiting the incredible amount of zooplankton in certain areas of the oceans, the whales of the sub-order *Mysticetes* lost their teeth and developed baleen. Baleen, growing in rows from the top of a whale's mouth like so many combs, is made of keratin, the same substance of which the human fingernail is made. This stiff but flexible comb-like arrangement functions as a filter or strainer, allowing water to pass through, while capturing small animals like small fishes, krill, or copepods. Filter feeding allows many whales to eat tons of food every day, all without teeth. In this ironic twist of evolution, the largest creatures on Earth feed on some of the smallest. The *Mysticetes* include whales like the Blue whale, Humpback, and Minke.

Within the *Odontoceti*, there are 10 families, of which 6 contain dolphins and porpoises. Most species fall into one of two families, *Delphinidae*, containing the oceanic dolphins and pilot whales, and *Phocoenidae*, containing the porpoises. The world's largest dolphin is the Orca, sometimes called the Killer whale. It reaches almost 10 metres in length and 8,000 kg.

The transformation from land animal to marine animal is perhaps nowhere more pronounced than in the body form of the cetaceans. All have assumed a hydrodynamic shape to allow the whales and dolphins to pass through the water with as little resistance as possible. Dolphins have long been the envy of scientists attempting to produce fast submarines with low drag. Some dolphins can swim at speeds of 40 kilometres per hour (30mph).

Left: A Short-finned Pilot whale surfaces for a breath, releasing an explosive lungful of air. The mist that sprays up doesn't come from within the animal, it's just water on the blowhole that gets sprayed when the whale exhales.

Anatomy and Senses

Dolphins are mammals like people, a class of vertebrates sharing many characteristics. Dolphins have lungs and breathe air. Like us, they will drown if they cannot get to the surface for a breath. But unlike us, they can hold their breath a long time. A Bottlenosed dolphin *(Tursiops truncatus)* can go 10 minutes or so without breathing, although they tend to breathe more frequently than that when possible. As well, we are both warm blooded, bear live young, and feed our young milk. We share other traits which go beyond simple taxonomy. We both care for and protect our offspring for a fairly long time. We both have a social system involving friends and families, and we both communicate with our own kind.

Opposite page: A pair of Bottlenosed dolphins approach me on a reef in the Caribbean. The scrapes on this animal's forehead are teeth marks from other dolphins. Sometimes dolphins rake each other with their teeth when they fight or play rough.

Above: A group of Spotted dolphins cavorting in the warm waters of the Bahamas.

Overleaf: A Young Atlantic Spotted dolphin, showing very few spots, releases a trail of bubbles as it vocalizes. Dolphins communicate with whistles and chirps. Certain sounds are accompanied by a tell-tale stream of bubbles.

Dolphins make squeaks and chirps, some of which we can hear when we swim with them. Biologists who study dolphin vocalizations have determined that each dolphin has its own personal squeak sound. When one dolphin calls out to another dolphin, it emulates the sound of the other dolphin. This is a dolphin form of calling each other by name. If this isn't impressive enough, consider this: if one dolphin calls out to another by name, then the other one must respond in some way, otherwise what would be the purpose of calling out to each other? Therefore, they must converse in some way. It is many people's belief that dolphins have their own language of squeaks and chirps, and talk to each other as we do with our language of words. While they certainly seem to make a lot of noise with their vocalizations at times, we have been unable to find conclusive evidence that they are in fact having conversations since we have no idea what, if anything, these vocalizations mean.

Above: An Atlantic Spotted dolphin hunting in the sand. The dolphin uses echolocation to "see" through the sand and find fish hidden below the surface. The dolphin makes clicks that penetrate the sand and bounce off of solid objects. The dolphin listens to the echo and finds the buried object.

Opposite page: Even though this water is extremely clear, many dolphins live in or visit murky water from time to time. Using echolocation, they can find their way without being able to see.

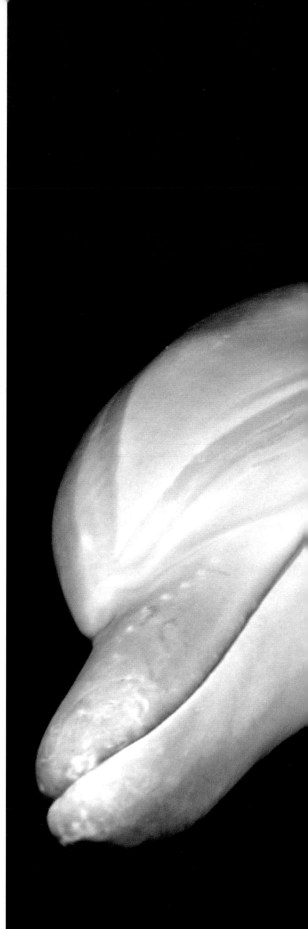

Since nobody has been able to decode the dolphin's "language" so we can understand it, some researchers have attempted to teach dolphins a language that both dolphins and humans can understand. Several researchers have taught captive Bottlenosed Dolphins sign language using as many as 60 different signs for nouns and verbs. Using this language, around 2,000 sentences can be constructed, and the dolphins understand every one of them. The research revealed that dolphins understand word order. In other words, they understand that "Take the ball to the ring" is different from "Take the ring to the ball." Very few animals can understand word order, the others being advanced primates like certain monkeys and gorillas. Unfortunately, the dolphins can't sign back to us, but we know they understand.

In a world where light doesn't travel very far, eyesight is very limited in its usefulness to dolphins. Although dolphins have excellent eyesight and can see well, theirs is a world of sound. Sound travels four times faster in water than it does in air, and it travels further too. Most dolphins navigate and hunt using their own form of sonar, called echolocation, which gives them a mental picture of an object, including its distance, size, location, density and thickness. The dolphin can even detect fishes hiding under a layer of sand. It sends out a series of clicks, then listens to the echo. Using highly evolved brainpower, the echoes allow the dolphin to "see" objects with sound.

Right: When the water is clear, dolphins use their excellent eyesight. This Bottlenosed dolphin is checking out the camera.

Research has brought insight into the dolphin's echolocation system. When we see an object with our eyes, we form a mental image in our minds of what the object looks like. Later, we can recall that image and match it to a picture or pick it out of a selection of other objects. But nobody knew how a dolphin would "see" an object with its echolocation. So, Dr. Louis Herman at the Kewalo Basin Marine Mammal Laboratory on Hawaii designed an experiment. In this experiment, a researcher places an object into an underwater box made of a frame covered in cloth. This box is transparent to the dolphin's echolocation, but opaque to it's eyes. The dolphin examines the object with its echolocation system. Finally, the dolphin is presented with two objects to examine out of the water with its eyes. In this way, the dolphin could not use its echolocation on the two objects. One of the objects is the same as the one in the box, and the other is different. Every time, the dolphin picked the right one, clearly indicating that the echolocation system of a dolphin forms an image in its brain the same way a visual image forms. So a dolphin can click away and literally see objects without using its eyes. But unlike vision, the echolocation system also penetrates the surface of objects. Dolphins can see through things and, like an x-ray machine, see the insides of objects. In fact, certain dolphins have been found to be able to differentiate between two materials whose thickness differs by only 1 mm (1/16th inch).

Above: A dolphin makes loud enough sounds to be heard both above and below water. When a Bottlenosed dolphin sticks its head out of the water, it can make loud clicks that can be heard by boaters.

Opposite page: A dolphin's fluke (tail) may not look like much, but the shape is optimized to produce a lot of thrust when coupled with a strong set of muscles to drive it. Some dolphins hit 50 kph!

The success of echolocation is dependent on some very advanced brain power. A dolphin has a large brain in comparison to its body, and complex as well. In fact, the brain of the Bottlenosed Dolphin is larger than a human brain. Although the dolphin's brain certainly must be large in order to process the complex echolocation signals they interpret, many biologists believe that the size of the dolphin's brain indicates a very intelligent animal. Unfortunately, dolphins, their senses and their environment differ so much from that of humans that we have a hard time imagining what their world, and thus their intelligence, is like.

It is a strange feeling to know that when a dolphin swims around me in the open ocean clicking its sonar system, it can see the air spaces in my lungs and probably see my heart beating as well. From just the way sound bounces off the swim bladder in a fish, a dolphin knows what kind of fish it is, without ever looking at its colour, shape or behaviour. In this way, dolphins can feed on fishes buried in the sand. They "see" through the soft sand, and find the fish they want to eat.

Previous page: Dall's Porpoise *(Phocoenoides dalli)* surfaces for a breath, Alaska. This cold water animal is hard to find. It usually surfaces at high speed, takes a quick breath and vanishes. It reaches a little over 2 metres in length.

Above: A young pair of Spotted dolphins have almost no spots. As they mature, they will gain more spots.

Obviously, such sonic acuity requires outstanding hearing. Although dolphins have tiny ear openings, scientists aren't sure if they are used, or if they are just vestigial leftovers from the past. Some biologists think they are still used for low frequency sounds, others think they do nothing. Scientists agree that most of the sound that gets to the ears of a dolphin are conducted through bones, specifically the lower jawbone.

The frequency range that dolphins can hear is much higher than our own. Human hearing ranges from roughly 20 Hz cycles per second to 20,000 Hz but dolphins hear from about 100,000 Hz to 150,000 Hz. Most of the sounds they make and hear are well above the range of human hearing.

Above: The Dusky dolphin (*Lagenorhynchus obscurus*) looks a lot like the Pacific White-Sided dolphin, but cannot be confused with it because their ranges do not overlap. This dolphin lives only in the south Atlantic and Pacific, around the coasts of South America, New Zealand and South Africa. These animals were photographed in the cool waters of Argentina.

Overleaf: One of the most acrobatic of all dolphins, the Long-Snouted Spinner (*Stenella longirostris*) often makes incredible leaps from the water. They are easy to identify because of the long, skinny rostrum (beak). This large group is on the move at sunset in Hawaii.

Dolphins have excellent eyesight, which is used in close range when the water is clear enough to see anything. The presence of rods and cones in the retina suggests that dolphins can see in colour, but colour vision in the ocean is not that important, since below about 9 metres (30 feet) there is very little colour to be seen without artificial light. (Water filters the colour out of the light, making everything seem like shades of blue). Dolphin eyes also have a well-developed tapetum lacidum, a light-reflecting layer behind the retina similar to that in a cat's eyes. It reflects light through the retina a second time, giving dolphins enhanced low-light vision. Considering that they often hunt at night and at dusk when there is little light, this low-light vision probably helps them a lot. Furthermore, dolphins can see independently with each eye. One eye can look one way, and the other eye can look another way at the same time. Humans use both eyes in the same direction to get a stereoscopic view of an object. Dolphins can look at two different things at the same time.

Below: Dolphins tend to be social animals. This pod of False Killer whales searches for food as a group. If they find something big enough, they will cooperate in catching it and share in the meal.

Opposite page: In the warm waters off Mexico, a Bottlenosed Dolphin approaches for a peek above the water at the strange guy with a camera.

Although dolphins seem to have a fairly well developed sense of taste, they likely have no sense of smell at all. Not only do they have no nostrils, but they have no olfactory lobes in the brain and no olfactory nerves. It seems scent is just not important to a dolphin.

A dolphin's blowhole, on top of its head, is used to breathe. It is connected to the lungs. The mouth, unlike humans, is not connected to the lungs and cannot be used to breathe. A dolphin typically just grabs a breath in a fraction of a second as it breaks the surface.

Dolphins are exceptionally powerful. In addition to being able to propel themselves through the water at amazing speeds, they can launch themselves out of the water in fantastic breaches. Some can attain heights of several body lengths. The fluke of the dolphin may not look like much, but it has a lot of muscle power behind it, and the shape is very efficient at pushing water.

A dolphin's flippers are not used for propulsion. They are mostly used to help the animal turn and manoeuver, like the ailerons on an airplane. They are also used to touch things, especially other dolphins. Dolphins are highly tactile. They often explore things by touching them, and they are often seen caressing and touching each other, most likely as a way of socializing.

Dolphins are highly evolved for their habitat and seem to be in complete control of their lives, masters of their realm. Their highly evolved senses and anatomy allows them to spend less time hunting for food than many other animals, and more time socializing.

Right: A group of Spotted dolphins with mixed ages shows the variation in spots. Older animals have more spots, younger ones have fewer.

Overleaf: An Orca patrols the waters of British Columbia in the afternoon. Its exhaled breath can be seen in the air as fine mist. It's powerful echolocation will lead it to food easily.

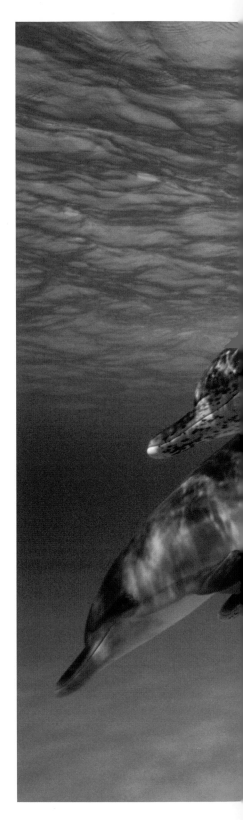

Social Lives and Reproduction

Unlike most other animals in the ocean, dolphins have social lives. There are a few theories on why this may be, but my theory is that dolphins are able to have complicated social lives because they have both the brain capacity and the time. While the majority of ocean creatures must devote a majority of their time hunting or foraging for food, dolphins do not. Their senses and hunting abilities, mostly because of their advanced echolocation, allow them to easily catch enough food without having to spend most of their time doing it. That leaves them with time for other things. Couple that with a large brain, and you have an animal that seeks mental stimulation. As a result, dolphins have become highly social animals.

Above: Pilot whales dive deep for their food consisting mostly of squid. They hunt at the edge of the continental shelf where they find the deep water and bottom topography that the squid like.

Opposite page: A Spotted dolphin slices through the water on its way to the bow of the boat for a free ride.

Dolphins are one of the few animals that invent and play games with each other, seemingly just for the fun of it. One such popular pastime that dolphins play is a game of "keep away". One dolphin will find a piece of seaweed or soft coral, and swim around with it, carefully balancing it across the front of a flipper, dorsal fin or fluke. (Rarely do they hold the object in their mouths). Other dolphins will attempt to steal this object away. Sometimes two dolphins will pass it back and forth, keeping it from a third animal. Sound familiar? This is the same game played by millions of school children with a ball on the schoolyard every day.

Years ago on my first trip to swim with wild dolphins in the Bahamas, I met captain Wayne Scott Smith who runs a dive boat and takes people out to swim with wild Spotted dolphins. With 20 years experience, Scotty is one of the most knowledgeable people I have ever met on the subject of wild dolphin behavior. He has spent literally years of water time playing with dolphins, and getting to know them. As a result, he has got to know many wild dolphins on a personal level. These animals recognize Scotty and his boat. They approach him closely, as if approaching a friend, and allow him access to their personal lives that few ever get to see.

Right: Dolphins often play with objects they find in the ocean as a means to entertain themselves. This Hector's dolphin *(Cephalorhynchus hectori)* is playing with a clump of kelp in the waters of New Zealand. The Hector's dolphin is one of the smallest dolphins, reaching only a metre and a half.

Many years ago he noticed the dolphins playing "keep away" with some seaweed, and thought it looked like fun, so he joined the game. Needless to say, a human being, no matter how good a swimmer he or she is, will never match water skills with a dolphin. There was no way Scotty had a chance of getting the seaweed away from any of the dolphins. But after tiring him out for a few minutes, the dolphins gave Scotty the seaweed and let him have a chance to engage in the game.

Since then, Scotty has often invoved his guests by actually initiating the game when he finds a playful pod of dolphins. He uses a brightly-coloured bandana which grabs the dolphin's attention. He jumps into the water from the back of his boat, and swims around, waving the bandana, until a dolphin takes interest and swims by to grab it. He then releases the bandana in the water, and the dolphin races away with it. The "bandana game" has begun. Now it is the job of the swimmers to try to get it back. Of course, if anyone manages to get the bandana back, it's only because a dolphin lets go of it on purpose. The dolphins will often tease the swimmers by swimming up just close enough that the swimmer can't quite reach. When the swimmer makes a move towards the bandana, the dolphin moves it again just out of reach. They clearly find it amusing to taunt the swimmers! Often the dolphins carry the bandana away to play amongst themselves and the bandana is never seen again. Other times, the dolphins play for a while, then let the swimmers have the bandana back, so the game can start over. Clearly, this is a case of an intelligent animal.

Above and opposite page: This series of images shows the "Bandana Game" in full swing. Captain Scott offers up a bandana to the dolphins. They take it and play 'keep-away' from each other and the divers. The animals can carry it on their fluke, rostrum or pectoral fins. Who needs hands?

Dolphins seem to have another social activity that keeps them busy: Sex. Dolphins are one of very few species of animals that have sex just for fun, not just for reproductive purposes. Even younger dolphins, not yet sexually mature, will practice mating. Many species of dolphins seem to exhibit a great deal of tactile behavior that goes with mating. For example, a male and female will swim close to each other, gently touching each other with their flippers as a form of foreplay. Sometimes foreplay is rough, involving raking teeth on each other. Many dolphins are seen with teeth scars from such activity. Once the actual mating begins, the animals swim belly to belly where the male will very quickly insert his penis into the female's genital slit. The whole thing is over in a few seconds.

The only way to determine a dolphin's gender in the wild is to get a good view of the underside of the animal. Males have two slits arranged like an exclamation point. The longer anterior slit houses the genitals, while the smaller posterior slit houses the anus. Females have one continuous slit which includes both the anal and genital openings. Females also have a set of slits containing the mammary glands, one on each side of the genital slit.

Right: Dolphins are tactile and love to touch and stroke each other, especially when they are in the mood for romance. This male Atlantic Spotted dolphin is trying to convince the female to mate with him.

Opposite page, top and above: These Atlantic Spotted dolphin pairs are mating, belly to belly. Dolphins are among the very few species on Earth that will mate just for fun as well as to reproduce. In fact, dolphins may mate many times a day!

Opposite page, bottom: A pregnant female Atlantic Spotted dolphin with a juvenile in tow. The juvenile is likely the female's previous calf. When she gives birth to the new calf, the previous one will be fully weaned and on its own.

Dolphins have a streamlined hydrodynamic body to swim efficiently through the water. Therefore, a male dolphin's penis and testicles are housed inside its body. On land mammals, the testicles are usually found outside the body to keep them cool, since sperm dies if it gets too warm. Dolphins have a special cooling system for their testicles. A network of blood vessels connects the testicles to the dorsal fin and flukes, drawing heat away from the testicles, and dissipating that heat on the thin surfaces of the fins.

Female dolphins have a bicornate uterus, meaning they have two internal reproductive sections that each act as a uterus. It may be an evolutionary link to their land ancestors. Their uterine system is similar to a horse or cow.

In spite of having what would appear to be the ability to have two calves at once (because of dual uteri), a dolphin tends to use only one uterus/ovary at a time. Dolphins almost always give birth to only a single calf.

Research indicates that a Bottlenosed dolphin's pregnancy lasts about 12 months. To save space, the calf's fluke and dorsal fin are folded over in the uterus. The calf is then born fluke first, with "creases" where the fins were folded. The creases go away after a few days. A Bottlenosed dolphin calf weighs about 13 kg and is about a metre long.

Once a calf is born, its mother will help it surface to breathe, but the calf is swimming on its own within minutes of being born. The mother will nurse the calf until it can catch its own food, which is usually about 2 years. Calves nurse about every twenty minutes or so, 24 hours a day. As they get older and learn to catch food, their dependence on milk lessens. Finally the calf is fully weaned and no longer needs milk. Within a year or so, the mother will mate again. Intervals between calves vary from about three to five years.

Left: A group of mixed age Spotted dolphins showing various spot development.

Overleaf: An Atlantic Spotted dolphin is starting to develop some spots. It's an adolescent. This animal is in a resting mode. Around mid-day, the dolphins often swim very slowly, half-asleep, resting for the night time feeding to come.

The calf has fringes along the edges of its tongue, believed to be an aid in nursing. The calf apparently rolls its tongue and clasps the fringes together to form a watertight funnel for the milk. Mothers take an active role in nursing by squirting the milk into the baby's mouth. The goal is to get the milk into the calf's mouth without any seawater – not an easy task.

Mothers often have the assistance of another female dolphin during birth. As well, mothers may pass their offspring off to another female to "baby sit" while the mother goes off to feed or rest. Males never participate in these rituals, nor do they have any role in the rearing of their offspring. Males in fact tend to stay together with other males most of the time, only socializing with the females when they are attempting to mate.

As the juveniles get a little older and start to gain their independence from their mothers, they often form their own little groups of juveniles. Here, even though they are not sexually mature, they will start practicing mating and feeding on their own, and the cycle begins again.

Right: Groups of young male Spotted dolphins often get together and go out to have fun. This is an important part of the dolphin social life. Boys will be boys.

Habitat

Dolphins live in virtually every aquatic habitat on Earth. While most dolphins live in the ocean, there are several species of river dolphins that live in freshwater in such places as the Amazon and the Ganges river in India.

We know the most about the Bottlenosed dolphin *(Tursiops truncatus)*, mostly because it has been the species most often kept in captivity for study, making it one of the more well-studied wild dolphins as well. The Bottlenosed dolphin is a single species, yet it can be described as having more than one "race" or ecotype. There is an ecotype that prefers coastal water, and another that prefers deeper, offshore water. They hunt in different ways and on different things. The coastal ecotype is adapted for warm, shallow waters. Its smaller body and larger flippers probably give it better manoeuverability and heat dissipation than the offshore ecotype. These dolphins frequent reefs, harbors, bays, lagoons, shallow coastal areas and estuaries.

Above: The Dusky dolphin loves to jump and play, and readily approaches boats to investigate and ride the bow wave. It reaches only 2 metres long.

Opposite page: The Bottlenosed dolphin on the left has survived an accident that left it disfigured. Dolphins are generally at the top of the food chain and almost nothing can mess with them and get away with it. Even sharks generally have no chance at making a meal of an adult dolphin. But when they are calves, dolphins are more vulnerable. So the sharks go after the calves.

Overleaf: Not all dolphins have the long, skinny rostrum associated with Bottlenosed dolphins. The Hector's dolphin has a more blunt face, and a striking color pattern that varies ever so slightly from one animal to the next. This dolphin is only found around New Zealand.

In general, the offshore ecotype seems to be adapted for deeper waters, where the temperature of the water will be cooler. Certain characteristics of their blood indicate that this animal may be better adapted for deep diving. Its larger body helps to conserve heat. The offshore Bottlenosed dolphin seems to eat mostly squid, caught at night in deep water.

The coastal Bottlenosed dolphin is more adaptable in what it eats – mostly fish and some invertebrates like shrimp. Some of the hunting techniques developed by these coastal dolphins are fascinating. For example, a group of Bottlenosed dolphins in Georgia and South Carolina, USA, have learned how to hunt near shore by driving a school of fish up onto a muddy bank. Called "strand hunting," a pod of dolphins cooperates to round up a school of fish. Then the dolphins drive the fish towards a muddy bank into shallow water. In their effort to escape, the fish swim into perilously shallow water, only a few inches deep. Then the dolphins take turns rushing in and splashing them ashore while beaching themselves in the process. The dolphin grabs a stranded fish or two as they flop on the mud, then wriggles itself back into the water. It's very clever, and only seen in a few places. This seems to be a hunting technique that the local dolphins discovered, then taught to each other. It gets passed down from generation to generation.

Above: Common, but shy, the Harbor Porpoise *(Phocoena phocoena)* strongly avoids divers. This rare photograph of one of the smaller dolphin species was made in Boston Harbor. It prefers cool, shallow coastal water.

Opposite page: Dusky dolphins love to jump and can leap several body lengths out of the water.

Spotted dolphins *(Stenella frontalis)* in the Bahamas tend to prefer the shallow sandy areas between the reefs during the day, where they frolic, rest and hunt in crystal clear water only 10 metres deep. But at night they become truly active and head towards the continental drop-off where they hunt squid in water several hundred metres deep. I will never forget an expedition where we headed out to the edge of the continental shelf one night, turned on all the big lights on the boat, and watched as the squid came to the lights.

Shortly thereafter, the dolphins came in to feed on the squid. I hopped into the water with a snorkel, at 1am in pitch darkness except for the lights of the boat, and watched as the dolphins whizzed past me to feed on the squid. It was spooky but incredibly exciting.

Opposite page: Spinner dolphins can jump several body lengths into the air, and love to spin around when they do it. One reason they might do it is to dislodge pesky remoras like this one.

Above: During the day, Spotted dolphins like shallow water where they play and sleep. At night they go offshore to find food in deeper water.

While tropical dolphins like Spotted dolphins don't tend to migrate, dolphins and porpoises that live in cooler waters often make migrations to and from their food sources. In summer, many species of temperate water dolphins will head towards the arctic (or Antarctic), where there is more plentiful food. But as winter approaches, the water will become too cold and they head back to warmer waters. There are many species of marine mammals, including toothed whales, that live in the arctic regions all the time, such as the Beluga whale or Narwhal, but these are technically not classified as dolphins even though they closely resemble them.

Most of the open ocean species of dolphins can dive very deep and hold their breath for longer than the coastal species, because they hunt in deep water. In the open ocean, much of the food is not near the surface but down several hundred metres, where there is a rich layer of zooplankton. The animals that survive on zooplankton live down there, especially squid. Under cover of night, this layer of animals moves closer to the surface, where the zooplankton can feed on the phytoplankton near the surface. The squid follow, and the dolphins dive to meet them.

From the sea to some freshwater habitats, from the tropics to the arctic and from the coast to the great reaches of the open ocean, dolphins have adapted to most aquatic environments on Earth.

Previous page: This Atlantic Spotted dolphin has a remora on its back. The fish hangs on with a dorsal fin that has evolved to work like a suction cup. The smooth skin of the dolphin makes a perfect place to latch on. Although the remora does not harm its host, its latch is irritating (I tried it!) and bothers the dolphin.

Right: Bottlenosed dolphins are wide-ranging in their habitats. Some prefer the shallower waters around the coast, while others prefer the deep water of the open sea.

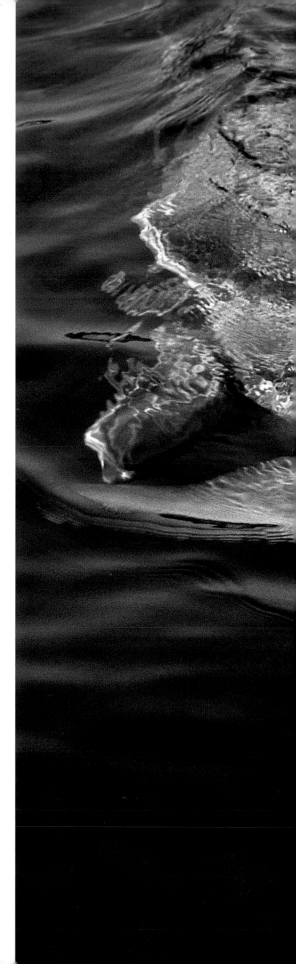

Dolphins and Man

Man has had a strange and evolving relationship with dolphins. In ancient times, many societies respected and even associated mystical powers with dolphins. They appear in artwork, pottery and even coins, going back thousands of years.

Today that respect is not as common. Dolphins are killed for food, put in aquaria for display, made to do tricks, and even slaughtered as a by-product of some fishing practices. Tuna purse-seining is probably the best known and infamous threat to dolphins in the world.

Above and opposite page: Because of their good disposition, high intelligence and friendly nature, Bottlenosed dolphins are the species most often kept in captivity and trained. Many feel that this practice is cruel.

For reasons not completely understood, dolphins and Yellowfin tuna often swim together, with dolphins closer to the surface and the tuna swimming beneath them. The tuna may be trying to take advantage of the dolphin's ability to find food, but it is also possible that the dolphins are following the tuna to eat what they eat. Fishermen have long known of the association between the two species and traditionally have used the dolphins to find schools of tuna. In the days when tuna were caught with hooks, this presented no threats to the dolphins. This changed dramatically when purse-seining was developed in the 1950's.

In purse-seine fishing, the fishermen find a pod of dolphins and surround the pod with huge nets that are over a kilometre (up to 1 mile) long and 100 metres (325 feet) deep. The assumption is that there are fish down beneath the dolphins. When the dolphins (and theoretically the tuna) have been completely surrounded, the bottom of the net is pulled closed, much like a drawstring purse. Purse-seining has proven to be an extremely effective method of catching fish. Entire schools of tuna can be captured very efficiently. Unfortunately, many dolphins are also killed in the process, as they become entangled in the nets and drown, or are crushed as the nets are hauled in. More than 20,000 dolphins are believed to die in purse-seine nets every year. The dolphins could hop right over the top of the nets to freedom, but for reasons nobody understands, they don't do it.

Opposite page: At a marine park, visitors get to pet a Bottlenosed dolphin. While some feel that this kind of attraction is valueless and demeaning to the dolphin, others feel that this kind of interaction gives people better understanding and respect for the animals.

Above: Although inquisitive and friendly, the Dusky dolphin doesn't make a good animal for captivity because it is just too active!

83

This method of fishing is especially predominant in the Eastern Tropical Pacific Ocean, a region which extends from southern California to northern Chile. Only certain species of dolphins, like the Spotted, Spinner and Common dolphins associate with tuna, and so they are the only species affected by this fishing technique. Tuna do not appear to associate with dolphins in other areas of the world.

In the early 1990's, environmental organizations began exposing this terrible fishing practice. Responding to public outcry, most tuna companies began labeling their tuna as "dolphin safe." Unfortunately, there was no standard and established definition for the term "dolphin safe." Some responsible tuna companies were in fact operating in a dolphin safe manner, while others used the slogan solely as a marketing tool as they went on killing dolphins. The public became increasingly skeptical about all claims of dolphin-safeness.

Previous page: In Roatan, Honduras, this pair of Bottlenosed dolphins live a 'semi-captive' life. They go out on the reef during the day to interact with divers who pay for the experience. But at night they go back into a pen where they are well fed and cared for. The owners of the resort claim that if the dolphins weren't happy, they could swim away at any time. It's hard to argue with that.

Left: A pair of Orcas spyhopping, a behaviour where the animals stick their heads above the water to have a look around. Orcas are curious animals and sometimes approach boats to investigate.

Overleaf: A snorkeler, even with a scooter, still has no chance of keeping up with a pair of Spotted dolphins, should they decide to take off. But the dolphins love the interaction with things new and different to them. The scooter always gets their attention.

In 1991, the United States passed a law that established a definition of "dolphin safe" and required tuna canners to meet certain minimum criteria before they could claim their tuna was dolphin safe in the U.S. Unfortunately, the "dolphin safe" criteria includes an annual allowable dolphin-kill quota, so it's really "dolphin safer" not "dolphin safe." Still this was a step in the right direction for dolphins. Even though most of the canned tuna available in Europe at the time did not come from these Eastern Pacific fisheries and was not caught using purse-seining on dolphin pods, the UK and Germany followed with similar dolphin-safe tuna laws.

Drift nets and gill nets also kill thousands of dolphins each year. The use of drift nets on the high seas was banned in 1993 through an international moratorium, but gill nets remain legal, and have now become the biggest killer of dolphins as by-catch.

Pollution has been a more recent cause for concern with dolphins. Pesticides, such as DDT, and industrial chemicals such as PCBs are getting into the ocean from runoff in higher and higher concentrations every year. Some of these chemicals are persistent, meaning that they accumulate in the tissues of animals that ingest them, and they move up the food chain. Dolphins and whales off the east coast of the United States and the west coast of the UK have the highest recorded levels of these chemicals in their bodies ever recorded in wild animals. Every year or so, a mass die-off of dolphins happens somewhere in the Atlantic ocean. Anywhere from a handful to hundreds of dolphins will wash up dead on the beach, the victims of chemical poisoning. These animals usually have PCB levels so high in their tissue, that they must be treated as toxic waste. What does this say about what we are doing to the habitat of our friends in the sea?

Compared to the plight of wild dolphins being killed in fishing practices or pollution, the issue of dolphins in captivity seems much less important. Yet many feel that keeping dolphins in captivity is cruel, not just because they are wild animals which don't want to be captive, but because of their sense of seeing the world. The dolphin's advanced echolocation enables it to "see" for great distances. It is thought that a dolphin can "see" with its echolocation for over 30 kilometres (20 miles). Putting such an animal into a swimming pool, no matter how spacious, would be like putting a person into a phone booth painted black. How can we expect an intelligent, social animal like a dolphin to be happy under such sensory-depriving circumstances?

Opposite page: A semi-captive dolphin performs a leap in his pen.

As a result, some dolphins don't survive long in captivity. A common problem with dolphins in captivity is suicide. Dolphins can get so depressed that they will intentionally sink and stop breathing. Unlike people whose breathing is automatic and controlled by the brain subconsciously, dolphins have to want to breathe and intentionally make an effort to breathe if they are to survive. They can drown themselves on purpose, and sometimes do.

However, dolphins kept in captivity serve as ambassadors of their kind. It can be argued that by keeping a few dolphins in captivity, we raise the awareness of thousands of people by allowing them to see dolphins up close, and learn how intelligent they are. Still, one wonders how training a dolphin to jump through hoops is raising awareness of the real plight that dolphins face to survive in the wild – avoiding fishing nets and not being poisoned to death.

We can only hope that in the future, humankind gets a handle on pollution and learns to respect the animals in the sea, even if they happen to stand between us and a school of fish. An ocean without dolphins would truly seem empty.

Left: A group of Atlantic Spotted dolphins approach me just as I have jumped off the back of the boat. For a few seconds I have their undivided attention while they figure out what I'm doing. After that, if I want to keep their attention, I'll have to work at it. The dolphins thrive on commotion. The more bubbles I blow and splashes I make, the more interesting they find my antics, and the less time I have for pictures!

Overleaf: Long-snouted Spinner dolphins are more known for their aerial displays than for their underwater antics. The dolphin on the left is pregnant, judging by her extended belly. She won't be doing many high jumps until she gives birth.

Other books in the *Wildlife Monograph* series

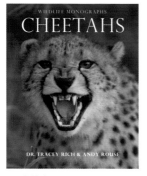

Wildlife Monographs –
Cheetahs
ISBN: 1-901268-09-8

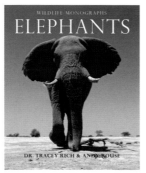

Wildlife Monographs –
Elephants
ISBN: 1-901268-08-X

Wildlife Monographs –
Giant Pandas
ISBN: 1-901268-13-6

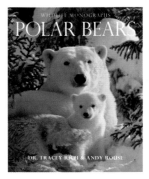

Wildlife Monographs –
Polar Bears
ISBN: 1-901268-15-2

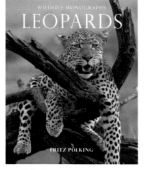

Wildlife Monographs –
Leopards
ISBN: 1-901268-12-8

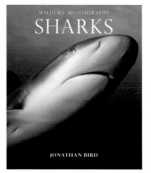

Wildlife Monographs –
Sharks
ISBN: 1-901268-11-X

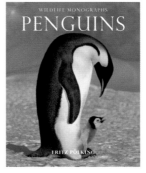

Wildlife Monographs –
Penguins
ISBN: 1-901268-14-4

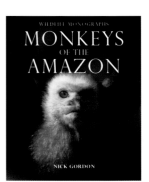

Wildlife Monographs –
Monkeys of the Amazon
ISBN: 1-901268-10-1

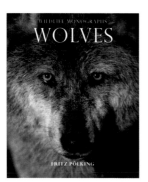

Wildlife Monographs –
Wolves
ISBN: 1-901268-18-7
        978-1-901268-18-8